SALLY ODGERS LISA STEWART

Australian Lullaby Treasury

A Scholastic Press book from Scholastic Australia

Scholastic Press
An imprint of Scholastic Australia Pty Limited
PO Box 579 Gosford NSW 2250
ABN 11 000 614 577
www.scholastic.com.au

Part of the Scholastic Group
Sydney • Auckland • New York • Toronto • London • Mexico City
• New Delhi • Hong Kong • Buenos Aires • Puerto Rico

Published by Scholastic Australia in 2025.

A catalogue record for this book is available from the National Library of Australia

ISBN: 978-1-76164-308-8

Typeset in Wilke, featuring Allura.
Illustrations created using watercolour, gouache, collage, rice papers and pencil.

We acknowledge the Traditional Owners of the Country on which we live and work.
We pay respect to Elders past and present.

Printed in China by Ink Asia.
Scholastic Australia's policy, in association with Ink Asia, is to use papers that are renewable and made efficiently with wood from responsibly managed sources, so as to minimise its environmental footprint.

10 9 8 7 6 5 4 3 2 1 25 26 27 28 29 / 2

ONE KEEN
KOALA
ABC

For Orlando and Sahara.—M.W.

For Frankie, who has the best laugh ever.—B.W.

Scholastic Press
An imprint of Scholastic Australia Pty Limited
PO Box 579 Gosford NSW 2250
ABN 11 000 614 577
www.scholastic.com.au

Part of the Scholastic Group
Sydney • Auckland • New York • Toronto • London • Mexico City
• New Delhi • Hong Kong • Buenos Aires • Puerto Rico

First published by Scholastic Australia in 2025.

A catalogue record for this book is available from the National Library of Australia

ISBN: 978-1-76164-239-5

Typeset in Lino Letter featuring Austral Slab.
The artwork in this book was created using watercolour on paper, and pencil.
Scanning by Klone Ltd.
Book design by Nicole Stofberg.

We acknowledge the Traditional Owners of the Country on which we live and work.
We pay respect to Elders past and present.

Printed in China by RR Donnelley.
Scholastic Australia's policy, in association with RR Donnelley, is to use papers that are renewable and made efficiently with wood from responsibly managed sources, so as to minimise its environmental footprint.

10 9 8 7 6 5 4 3 2 1   25 26 27 28 29 / 2

ONE KEEN KOALA ABC

MARGARET WILD BRUCE WHATLEY

A Scholastic Press book from Scholastic Australia

A

One Keen Koala, all **ALONE . . .**

'Will you play with me?'

But **BILBY'S** bumping down a slope.

CROCODILE'S

swinging on a rope.

Emu's

DANCING

on her toes.

ECHIDNA'S

making gumleaf bows.

Glider's **FISHING**
in the creek.

GOANNA'S

playing
hide-and-seek.

Wombat's twirling a **HULA HOOP.**

Magpie's making
INCHWORM soup.

Kangaroo's
JUMPING
in a puddle.

KOOKABURRA
wants to cuddle.

Penguin needs
a **LITTLE** nap.

Bandicoot's
found a
treasure
MAP.

NUMBAT
wants to try
to write.

OWL is busy
flying a kite.

POSSUM'S
painting a
scary face.

QUOKKA'S

ready to run a race.

Lizard's
READING
a book with
Mouse.

SEAL is building
a cubbyhouse.

TIGER QUOLL'S

making a golden crown.

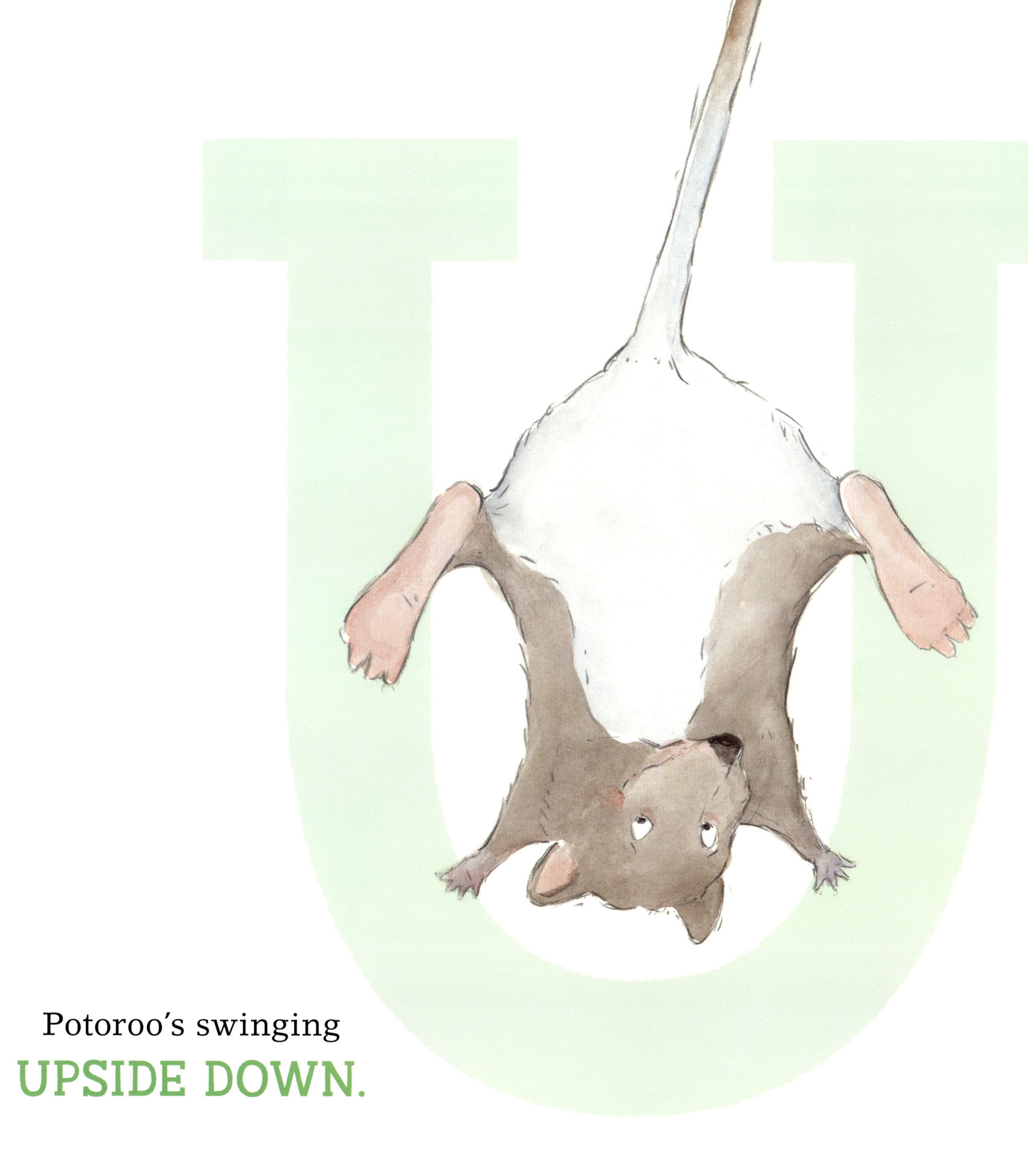

Potoroo's swinging

UPSIDE DOWN.

Cockatoo's
playing the
VIOLIN.

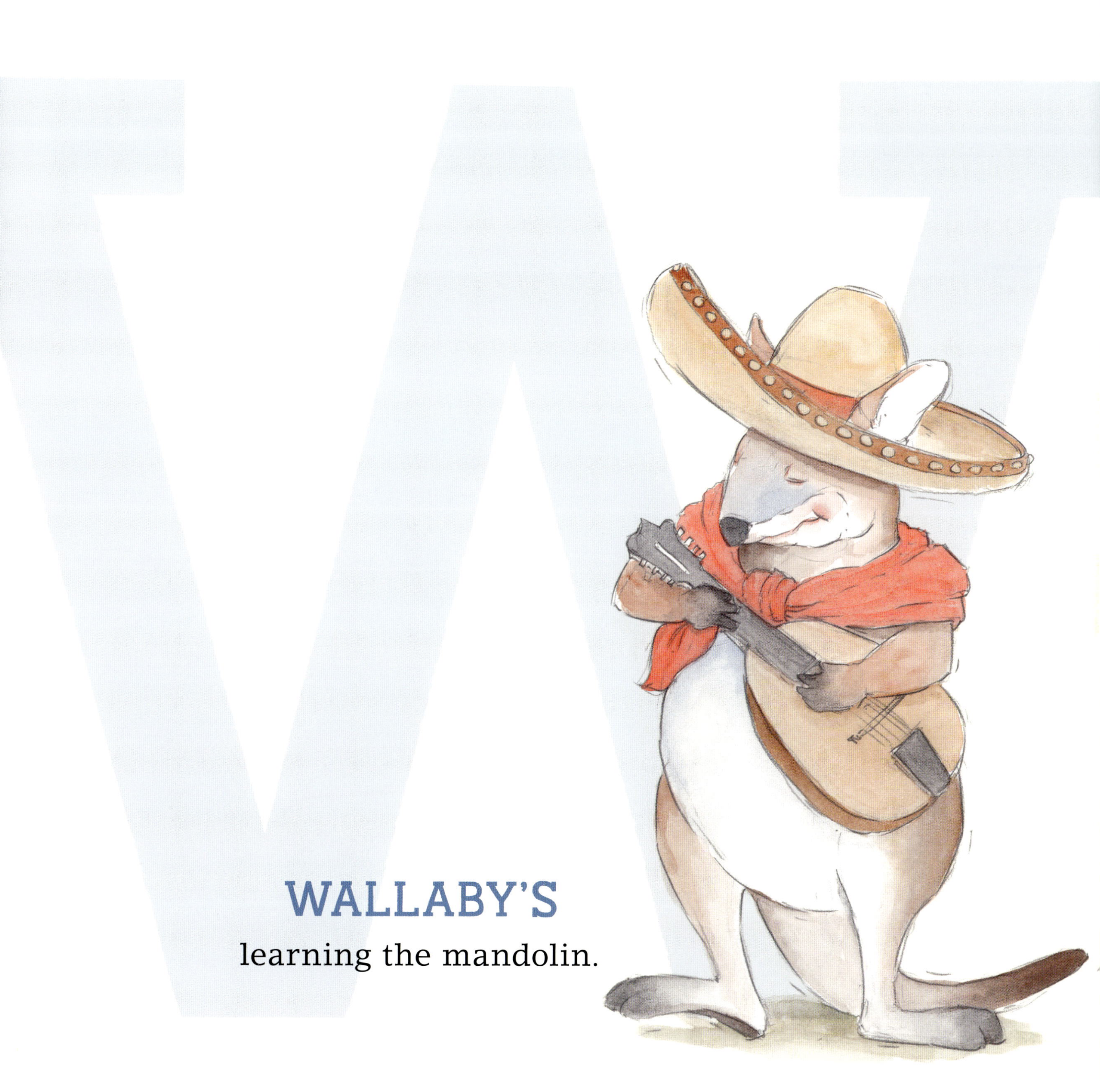

WALLABY'S

learning the mandolin.

Dingo's
chasing after
FOX.

YABBY'S

sailing in a box.

One Keen Koala, all alone.

'Will you play with me?'

And, at last . . .

ZEBRA FINCH says,
'Woohoo!
I'd love to play
with you!'